CAPE POETRY PAPERBACKS

TED WALKER
FOX ON A BARN DOOR

Ted Walker

FOX ON A BARN DOOR

POEMS 1963-4

JONATHAN CAPE

THIRTY BEDFORD SQUARE LONDON

FIRST PUBLISHED 1965
REISSUED IN THIS FORMAT 1969
© 1965 BY TED WALKER

JONATHAN CAPE LTD
30 BEDFORD SQUARE, LONDON WC1

SBN 224 61774 5

Printed in Great Britain by
Fletcher & Son Ltd, Norwich
and bound by
Richard Clay (The Chaucer Press) Ltd, Bungay, Suffolk

Contents

Acknowledgments

The poems 'By the Saltings', 'Break-waters', 'Skimmers', 'Estuary', 'The Skate Fishers', 'The Burning', 'By the Bridge', 'Carp', 'Rook Shoot', 'Star-lings' and 'Mushrooms' appeared origi-nally in the *New Yorker* (© 1963 and 1964 The New Yorker Magazine, Inc.).

Most of the other poems in this volume have appeared before. Thanks are due particularly to: *Encounter*, the *Observer*, the B.B.C. Third Programme, the *Poetry Review*, the *Listener*, *Priapus*, *The Times Literary Supple-ment*, *Stand*, *Outposts*, the *London Magazine*, the *Transatlantic Review* and the *Critical Quarterly*.

For
LORNA
and
OUR CHILDREN

Fox on a Barn Door

By the Saltings

When the wind is in the thrift
gently, down by the saltings,
at dawn when the vapours lift;

and pattering sanderlings
run from you rather than fly
across the sandflat screaming;

before the runnels drain dry
among the sea-lavender
and sun severs sea from sky;

there is time enough, under
any listing low-tide hull
of your choosing, to wonder

at the force of it to pull
you to its shelter, alone
as you are and as fearful

as some crab beneath some stone.

Breakwaters

Elms are bad, sinister trees.
Falling, one leaf too many,
they kill small boys in summer,
tipped over by a crow's foot,
bored with the business of leaves.

An uneasiness attends
dead elms — timber for coffins,
ammunition boxes. And
breakwaters. Bolts open sores
of orange rust in their flanks,

and yet there is loveliness.
Ultimate green of eelgrass
soothes with the comfort of hair
all the tiny agonies
that crawl in hidden places

and sing when the tide is low
and death is not imminent,
scrabbling in an eczema
of pink and white barnacles
and mussels of midnight blue.

Terrifying as altars
by night, black, a sea-Stonehenge.
Filigrees of little wracks
dance on them at high water
in a devil-dance. They change.

Their male look lasts a few tides;
when the reek is washed away
and the stubble is shaven,
on a tall September night
the sea will take his new brides.

In his calm he will lap them,
then batter their waists away,
emphasize their Celtic heads.
And when they are old and raddled,
thin, thin as a Belsen arm,

they will stand bare and skinny
and their stringent, hard old hearts
will disregard his knocking.
Dour, malignant to the core,
they will try to outlive him.

Skimmers

When the sun begins to throw
between boulders darknesses
and the skimmers gather shells
at the edge of amber pools,
he follows his long shadow
through the sea-wall buttresses.

He stands by the longest groyne
in a black and tattered coat,
watching a boy make a mound
of oyster shells on the sand,
hurl them up the wind and on,
curving, curling, lying flat

in the windwall, falling fast
to the dark Decembered bark
that lists by the low-tide mark.
Too old for the skimming now,
still he advises, will boast
of the skill he once had, how

as a boy he used the wind
to lob a cockle over
trees as high as a rook flies.
So he flings his memories
again and again, never
disbelieved. His tales soar and

are caught awhile in the breath
of a boy's brief innocence.

When he comes here wanting death
but not the dying of it,
watching wind in water
white in the seas of winter,

his eyes weep truths of summers
when crops of poppies were blown
like paper parasols back
and wings of yellowhammer
hovered on the white chalk rock.
And when he moves on alone,

shuffling up the pea-beach track
on shores of his mind's making,
he does not stop to look back
at the long rollers breaking;
or at the boy that he knows
at a distance follows.

Estuary

As the image of the sun
after the blinding moment
lasts on the closed lids violet
an instant, and colour comes
across the tight eye's darkness
though the source of light has gone,

so when I take the low lane
between the fields of barley,
with the slither of a sea-
wind sucking the sun-cracked husks,
to gaze at the sunken hulks
of ships as they flake at noon

in the lapped inlet, I can
recall that, with the tide-race
of boyhood just begun, once
I ran down the jetty steps,
stubbing up pebbles, and stopped
to stare at a bark broken

in three across the open
mudflat, each part with a mast
still and splintering spars, fast
in banks of sand: and though I
remember the terror my
eyes saw treading the decks on

that bright morning with the wind
light now — the wind that had smashed

that great ship fallen, awash
like driftwood, ribbed in fitful
patches of water — yet still
I would wish to be alone

with the loneliness of then;
and free to make my horrors
walk the boards beyond the shore
at the bidding of my will
only; with the power, as well
as to make, to efface them

by turning to see the men
with bright bandana faces
gladdening the noonday as
they picked the purple winkles
like scatterings of damsons
with salt dried like bloom on them.

Porpoises

Sometimes in summer the sea
looks infrangible; dull steel
dimpled like a dinner-gong.
The metal may be pitted
at the far rim with the hulk
of a forty-foot basker.

A sudden clap-trap of gulls —
and mackerel-magnetized
the sea scribbles lines of force
to attract crazed porpoises
frantic with feeding and rut
close to an inshore bather.

The cow gives suck as she rolls
through her bull's parabola,
dragging her calf over groynes
in his wake of white lather:
and her broad, round head tumbles
to his rhythm. Her thick lips

curl like a negress's lips.
When she dives her flukes lie poised
on the surface an instant
as she breaks another back
among the perfervid shoal
with an automatic snap

of appalling, fluted jaws.
The herd is sleek and wanton,

frenzied, intent as athletes;
paced by herring, hulls of ships,
they never stop, never sleep.
They copulate on the move.

And sometimes, along the shore,
you come across one stranded
like a great, obscene, black slug.
Age, exhaustion, impotence,
but no disease can kill them.
They die when they fall behind.

Baby Ling

This often happens at neap tide.
I'd poked about for mussels on the groyne;
Toyed with stubborn limpets.
Hidden in the moist, maidenhair fringe
You cringed where barnacles sing their gritty song
Alongside crabs, cohabiting with soft-back crabs
And scabbed anemones.

Seizured, you sprang from your safe cleft;
You left unlovely fellows stranded,
Landing at my feet and at my feelings.
Heeling is good enough for you.
To be heeled is the penalty for ugliness.

But I did the decent thing and left you alone;
Only watched your wretched effort to escape,
Shaking all your tiny, ragged strength
The length of the wet sand.

And yet you didn't reach the balm of water:
You expired, short of ten yards' strength.
A canny whitebait would have sandplunged;
Flounders would have camouflaged;
Soft-back crabs remained occult and breakered, clefted.
But you failed at every turn.

                                                And
Gulled with this false shriek of guilt
I felt your death was purposeless and trite;
I might as well have spared my feelings,

By heeling you.

The Skate Fishers

Now, as at its first shining,
Saturn burns slow and alone
to rise on a sudden night
in time for a tide neaping
to an imminent full moon,
they come to their boats and light

their lamps. Propitious the sound
of the suck and the gunwale's
rough rub on the quay-wall stone,
the dry deck strewn with dry sand,
no wind fingering it nor swells
to roll one grain away. Then

offshore, no boards creaking, still
amid stillnesses of sea,
the long throb of engines stopped,
they must wait a while till
indigo water and sky
violet have interlocked.

Nine such nights a year only
they have, and some must be missed,
when they may pay a line low
to the grey scabbed skate that lie
among the boulders buttressed
in, nine nights only to pay

a long line down at the mark
that needs such calm to be found

and held. But when the ratchet
clatters, when a kittiwake
disturbed rises, when, entwined
in weed, line hisses, at that

taut instant the great skate dives
through his black rock canyon
deep, deep, beating his wide wings
on its walls; on, on through caves
of no man's knowing. Upon
some arcane ledge, huge, he hangs

pulsing with irritation.
And with each heave of him pumps
the rod above and sideways,
fretting the tightened line on
a jutting shelf till it snaps.
The men, like petrels, restless,

move on across the surface,
veined and broken, through the stars'
shattered images to shore;
and the skate, with a grimace
of torn lip, spits blood, and goes
to do a killing elsewhere.

Lancing Beach

An asphaltic sea had lain
with a rash of bladder-wrack
breaking out along its back.

It was a sea-leukaemia
and the sea convulsed with it,
throwing up silver brit

and the body of a man.
Here it was they found him, here,
with little eels in his hair,

and from his unstoppered husk
fluid flowed. Balls of black flies
rolled in the pits of his eyes.

I flung a great pearl of grief
with all my strength at the sea's
apathy. Polycrates

soon had his precious pearl back.
The rings I made would not reach
to break on that other beach:

the grief I cast was for me;
lest I lie dead on this sand.
Lie dead. In this no-man's-land

each stone's a necropolis.
An orthodox death. Absurd
to speak comfortable words.

The grief I cast is for me.
There is a smell of sickness —
I must come to terms with this.

On the Sea Wall

Attending the First Coming,
expecting that some shudder
of Him should pulse here under
me stronger than the knocking
sea that throbs through the greenheart,
I wait for a faith to start
shaking me. Again nothing

stirs. But I stay, lest I miss
beyond the mind's wall, where are
distances that never star
was adequate to express,
some comet fall of insight
in the chasm of this night
to light me my loneliness.

Conger

An hour since, you lay coiled in your inheritance;
The broken spars of a sunken Spanish orange-boat,
The manor you won when you weighed a mere forty
    pounds.
There you lived alone, eating all spies and intruders,
Hidden down among the cold, chryselephantine stones.

You have teeth like the spikes on a barrel-organ drum:
That necrologic gape closed its horny doors of knives
On the hebete like the Iron Maid of Nuremberg.
You have the limbless streamlining of the latest cars.
Your tiny scales are apt, like a wrestler's tiny eyes.

Now you lie dead. On the bottom boards you lie dead.
This is how things should be.

Under the Pier

He has a bargain who buys
the cheap, comfortable lies
they are selling on the pier.

Inside the Hall of Mirrors
you can buy cut-price horrors:
little men with chorea

will dance for you. The Ghost Train
always brings you back again
from Hell. And you're always near

an emergency exit.
You're entitled to forget
crude facsimiles of fear —

you pay to. It's free down here
to look at the old dead-beats
who lie embalmed in their sweat

without will enough to leer
at the couples doing what
they can against the wall. Not

an urge left in them, they're
waiting till it's time to go;
they'd die, but don't know how to.

This is how things are. Nothing's
unnatural that happens.
They lie in the night and hear

the barkers up on the pier
cry dummy death for the tasting.
Down here the kicks are lasting.

Harvest Moon

Wafer of altar-bread, the moon,
white, round, brittle at the edge.
In a wisp of fibre soon
September-priest takes bread; at ledge
of sky, the chalice lip, in flood
of sunrise dips the moon in blood.

Erosion

There have been
such times before; times when rain
has seemed ceaseless and the clay
has slipped like this, endlessly
away.

We have known
days like these when it seemed sun
would come alien to our eyes
if again it came to us
as once:

when we hoped,
when at last the rains had stopped,
we would learn some way to bear
the weight of so much water;
endure

one more time
if it came, and it has come,
the sight of the sodden clay
as it slips like this, endlessly
away.

The Burning

The stubble burning began
today, fire tonguing furrows
where lately the rats had run
that now, with pheasant and gull,
skulk among rusting harrows
at field-edge out of the pull

of funnelled winds. With the flames'
peremptory signatures
to the season's ending came
a flaked ash of cirrus wisp
tonight, multiple fractures
of yellow trees, a last wasp

kindled in the hips, berries
that cracked in the red spindles
and a thin wind that carries
yet detonations of jays'
wings as the last light dwindles
below the branch-line of yews.

And in the burning fields now
the images are changing.
Sometimes the fires are a row
of children's sunlit faces,
round, in yellow hair tumbling;
or, as a night breeze rises

on a sudden, a saw edge
surging jagged through the straw,

ripping from hollow to ridge
a whole furlong. Tomorrow
will come plovers and jackdaw
flocks to pick a living through

the desolate acres. Oaks,
leafless, will be as thumb-prints
smudged on the sky; rains will soak
each last, cold cinder away.
A sense of panic, no plants
left to grow, strengthens as clay

sweats, cooling. I would wish
the fires to burn a while more,
fruits not to fall from the bush
a while more, nor I to pass
by, till the slate-shine shives are
cut for the coming of ice.

By the Bridge

I recall, before the banks
sank in this wilderness of rains,
clear waters of the Wild Brooks
torrented atop white rocks
worn smooth and slabbed, with a sun
in bubbles splintered over them.

I stood on this bridge and saw
the waters mix; the confluence,
too, of sparrows and shadow
the length of the long hedgerow;
and finches strung on fences
like bright beads on an abacus.

There were sounds of quietness
not listened for, but heard
among beds of watercress
where, with eyes of gentleness
and hocks sucking soft hot mud,
some patient herd always waded.

Every close-cropped pasture, lush
with marsh-marigold, was quiet
with an intermittent hush
of leaves in a delicate ash
when the wind unentwined
and not a cricket fidgeted.

Whatever the stream bore down
from unaccountable hills

in the misted distance, passed on
to gaze at dark reflections
in the deep blue calm of pools
below the drop of the falls.

All ugliness, all violence
passed away. Through the stone piers
of the bridge's permanence,
uprooted trees in remonstrance
brushed eely green streamers
of silkweed, pulled to the weir

beyond. Even when the great storm
broke, massive banks drained
vast cargoes away; but a dam
of blackened branches jammed
across the stream and all poured
over. Still the lands lie under flood

and no quietness of sound
is heard now in the silence
seeping from the vanished ground.
Violated, broken things find
islands to rot upon. The dance
of the multiple suns is done.

Carp

By day falls the white blossom
of may on his olive back
inert on top like a rock.
Small silver shiners spin from
him as bright jangles of fry
veer from his stillness. But by

night, when bats bring their darkness
and start to sip at the pool
in a sideslip as they whirl
round the same two trees endlessly, come the night skirmishes.
He has been waiting for this.

It is as though night prises
a scale or two up. He bolts
through reeds to smoothen them; halts;
sucks the yellow irises
encrusted with yellow eggs.
He sucks till his belly sags,

as he quaffs in unison
with the cows' rough tongues ripping
grass at the edge. His sipping
admits a long procession
of passing flies. Then it stops.
He turns within his length, flaps

a gossamer from his fin,
and, exploiting his great strength,

hurls his amplitude the length
of a pond too small for him,
back and back and back again,
savaging the restriction

of lily stalks and the roots
where the lurking yellow perch
hover in amazement, arch-
ing their spines. And he starts
circuiting, circuiting, like
a brash skater at a rink,

trailing his barbels beneath
his gape as he goes, rejoic-
ing that he was made for this
alone, until the first breath
of a day breeze blows and quiet-
ly he attends a new night.

Grebe

Today the April winds blow
in the tippets of your crest;
the waves are hard beneath you,
as by your will. And you stand
wide-winged like a little Christ
using the water like land.

I can forget the mammal
that I am for days; and though
in the womb I was reptile,
fish, I have no memory
of the scales I shed, and no
sense of the gekko in me.

But you — are you going back
to be again what once you were
before your ancestors shook
their first wet feathers and flew
into the alien air
you find so alien now?

Cuckoo-pint

So cold now. I remember
you — bright hedgerow tarts you were,
flagrant in your big red beads,
cheerful, vulgar and brazen.
But then,

in a sudden October,
when the white night of winter
came, you put aside your gauds
and took vows. Now you open
again,

hooded, cool and sinister.
I know you for what you are
unveiled: loose, secular brides
frustrated with this convent
torment.

Rook Shoot

Against the evening light, strung
across banks of cumulus,
goitres of mistletoe hung
from the necks of poplars.
Higher, in elms, rookeries
knotted the topmost traceries,
rank and black like a cancered lung.

Always a restlessness turned
in the top of those tall trees:
even at rest the birds leaned,
lurching backwards as a breeze
blew fitful into their faces
scabrous with the rub of branches
jabbed. There was no comfort

up in those crowded tenements,
save the warmth sometimes of sun
cupped in Aprilled-out softness
of new leaves, barely green,
that soothed for a while the roughness
away. At a time of this
tenderness, the men came.

Quickly they did what they had
come to do. They had no need to kill,
but some part of them remembered
the need of a man to kill
and had brought them with their want
under the purple birds. They shot.
And one by one the dark parcels fell,

thudding, to cumber the ground
underfoot, twitching out the last
frenetic beat of wing and heart.
We, when the men had passed
on, stood a while to watch
some turning birds in the distance
gyrate nearer, nearer, land

indomitable under
the ravage, walk among
the spilt eggs, peck them, gather
sustenance enough to sing
a cracked, ragged song up in
the roomier trees, to begin
tomorrow a new growth all over.

Disused Canal

Earth began to take it back
years, years before men left
it; and their horses, put to pasture,
trailed their manes in the softness of fern fronds; years, before
their long, brass-bound barges sank
to glint among the kingcups.

No sooner were they opened
for the first time, these locks —
and the only rush ever
of a wall of water shook
each bridge, quiet over
stagnancy since — than dormant
seeds in the clay bed sprouted,

never to be put down, bled
once a year and strengthened by
bill-hook. The hold tightened;
banks grew close with tufty
hummocks. Then rose the silted
bottom through the water and
once again the land won back

the length of cut. A thick
scum of duckweed only lies
where a man might have stood once,
and still have drowned. Only flies,
with the drug of dusk, now dance
to an oriental music
where the bargees sang to the hooves.

There are places where no weed moves
ever, now, when a wind blows:
there will come a time, and soon,
for the shrivelling of willows
and for the last flocks of down
to toss like gondolas on waves
from a swan's swooping. And

when the final crumb will have dried
and the fissures of June have scarred
parched patches where no grass
will grow, they will come once more,
the men, to turn back earth
encrusted with the sun and wind,
hard as they and as obdurate.

Song in the Night

Once we slept
when it was done:
though with wanting you

I sometimes wept
you a tear or two
more,

the night half gone.
I never saw
the stars move then

as they move now,
now it is done,
passing the window

glistening
in my eyes till morning
as you sleep

and I weep
through
wanting you.

Old Couple

We know no other daylight now,
except such little as may lie
along dark folds of drapery

mornings, evenings, the sun low
enough to find a shafted way
to us through a bolted window.

Little enough there is left
for us to need between the sun
of morning after we have lain

long, and sun of evening, soft
on the folds, before once again
we lie out all the night bereft

of sleep, thought, sensation. A bed
is all we have to own, to know
the limits of our limbs in; grow

a little feebler in. No need
remains for us, save only to
sense when one of us is dead

when the one of us will be dead.

Song for my Children

When you pulled me to
the waterside,
wanting me to throw
stones at the great grey bird,

my face so scolded
you, there was no
need for words. You cried.
And in your thoughts you threw,

little children, at
me, all your fear
of the bird forgot-
ten. Sometimes I come here

to meet my fear by
the dark water;
gain ascendancy
with a quick small kill. Your

candid eyes will cloud
soon, raked by know-
ing what I have told
with mine today. But how —

when you pull my face,
little children, to
meet your candid eyes —
how shall I lie to you?

Terrains Vagues

At the edge of any town
and the edge of any life
are tracts we never build on;
ragged wildernesses, half-
wild, unkempt and overgrown.
They're easy to return from

and there is no risk. Children,
gipsies, lovers, tramps, all go there
to do what they must: and none
can come to harm, save when we're
there too. For we infect them
with our coming. When we stare

at them, steal a turf or two,
litter them with what we've felt,
they are soiled by what we do
and they watch us with our guilt.

Visitation

The properties conventional to fright —
Judgments of attitudinizing owls
Pronounced among the armadillo cowls
As liquid dusk coagulates to night;

A snowstorm imminent, with flecks of white
Fritillaries congealed and smoothed by trowels
Of ululating winds; the dog that howls
In an adjacent street. The scene is right,

If hackneyed. Can a bullet not quiesce
The owl, another kill the dog? Suns rise,
The mornings come, the snows must deliquesce.

But there's that God I won't believe in. And
The dumb insolence I see in his eyes
Leaves me as scoured as a worm in sand.

Starlings

Our fears, like starlings, gather
with the dusk. Small particles
they come, innumerable,
flying direct from further
skies of mind only guessed at.
Wheeling, they circle us, squat

near. If ever a pair of birds
should strut a sunlit pavement
before us, caught in movement
of the day's concern, we goad
them, approach, put them to flight;
sometimes, even, feed them. But

lodged, untouchable by night,
in the high clerestories
of the stone-still, moon-carved trees
we move among, they will not
be put up at our passing
boldly under their roostings.

Sometimes we can keep away
through the long-lain night. Awake
we may avoid them, though flocks
heave throbbing through our dreams, high
in the misproportioned limbs
of our imaginings.

If we should decide to come
to them, hear their mummeries

mock us when one of them stirs
to ripple through all of them,
sacristan black, we may judge
their strength, though they will not budge

before the day. When they go
they leave uneasy calm, as
they turn as one like louvres,
letting the sunlight through.
And only the sense remains
of the black beneath the sheen

and the knowledge that the swift
and silent flight of other
birds, unseen, has passed over
us, sinister, borne aloft
by wings more menacing
yet than those of the known starling.

Mushrooms

By three spindle-trees, far from
the far stars once in a dream,
in a dream I stood alone
beneath a varicose moon
that hung by the Little Wood
still. And though no wind had blown

that night, yet the bulrushes
swished and the parching grasses,
sibilant with the hustle
of dry vipers, were alive
with scales. I ground the pestle
of each tree-top as I moved

into the moon's mortar, fled
through aspens where fear quivered
me still from the lisping fields,
until, exhausted, I fell
among mushrooms and lay cold
with the shudder of them all

about me. I watched them grow
with a shuffle of mould through
dead leaves, taking the colour
of the night that conceived them,
pink and brown in the pallor
of a falling-flecked moonbeam,

black in the shadow of roots.
And in that flicker of plants,

only the nightshade I knew
by name, knew that its berries
would fall and die where they grew
and poison drain away. Those

other growths — unkillable,
teeming coolie-caps, fungal
infections on an oak-bark,
all the fine spores that I breathed
that night — live on in the dark
wildernesses of my mind,

and they will lie a long age
inactive there till I reach
once more and unwillingly
those three spindle-trees far from
sleep — trees that once before I
saw in a dream, in a dream.

Easter Poem

I had gone on Easter Day
early and alone to be
beyond insidious bells
(that any other Sunday
I'd not hear) up to the hills
where are winds to blow away

commination. In the frail
first light I saw him, unreal
and sudden through lifting mist,
a fox on a barn door, nailed
like a coloured plaster Christ
in a Spanish shrine, his tail

coiled around his loins. Sideways
his head hung limply, his ears
snagged with burdock, his dry nose
plugged with black blood. For two days
he'd held the orthodox pose.
The endemic English noise

of Easter Sunday morning
was mixed in the mist swirling
and might have moved his stiff head.
Under the hill the ringing
had begun: and the sun rose red
on the stains of his bleeding.

I walked the length of the day's
obsession. At dusk I was

swallowed by the misted barn,
sucked by the peristalsis
of my fear that he had gone,
leaving nails for souvenirs.

But he was there still. I saw
no sign. He hung as before.
Only the wind had risen
to comb the thorns from his fur.
I left my superstition
stretched on the banging barn door.